William Collins Sons & Co Ltd
London · Glasgow · Sydney · Auckland
Toronto · Johannesburg

Also compiled by Nanette Newman
GOD BLESS LOVE

Cover and endpaper designs
by Sarah and Emma Forbes

First Published October 1974
© Byran Forbes Limited 1974
Reprinted 1976
ISBN 0 00 195288 9
Made and Printed in Great Britain by
William Collins Sons & Co Ltd Glasgow

LOTS
OF
LOVE
x

We love you we don't hate you

A collection of children's sayings
compiled by
NANETTE NEWMAN

COLLINS St James's Place, London

Loving is the first thing
children learn –
I wish life would teach
them never to forget it.

Nanette Newman

I caN speak French.

I caN say Paris.

Jane aged 5

all my clothes have had other people in them

Paolo aged 7

My mother ses she's cold and then she makes me put on a coat

Colin aged 7

why do all those fhootballers
kiss each other on the Telly.
theyre not married
theyre not even
engaged,

Jason aged 6

when I am at school my mummy
haz fun

Stephen aged 5

I love my mother because
i have a Photograph of her
and she sends me presents.

Paul aged 7

When you are a baby
you can see your
mummys bosum but
When you grow up its
not alowed and I think
thats a silly rule,

Vivienne aged 6

I love my daddy becorse he give me a good ejukashun

Zoe aged 6

When my daddy was driving his car we saw a fox lying in the road and nobody stopped. you should always stop and say goodbye to dead things.

Liz aged 8

Women do the washing up and cleaning and tidying and men go on the train and get tired.

Penny aged 7

I LIKE this

I've got three daddys which is nice

at birthdays but not at other times

Elena aged 5

My mummy sais I must love evreyboddy even the peple who killed my daddy but I dont.

Helen aged 7

Me Dad went to prison and we have to keeps remembring to love him

Jean aged 7

You couldn't make everyone in the world love each other. They dont even get on in blocks of flats.

Lois aged 7

Babees need to be loved by
their mother in case
evrybody hates them when they
grow up.

Norman aged 7

You have to love your own
baby because everyone else
finds them a newsance.

Patrick aged 8

Babys
Don't
grow
On Trees

IF a baby dropz out of yourtummy When your zhopping You must ring the police.

Deborah aged 6

My Teecher is very crule. She smaks Peple all day and she eats frogs legs and maks cros spells. I dont like her becos she says I tell fibs.

David aged 6

I hayt scool and scool lunches and the teecher and all my friends.

Patrick aged 6

my mother has witish yelleow hare. pinkish eyes and lots of Teeth and she Is very brtifvll.

Ann aged 6

When you are a baby your mother feeds you from her boZom but She can only do milk.

Felicity aged 7

You shoud never help a baby to walk becaus. It falls down and cuts its knee and you always get a smack.

Cormac aged 6

We went to peter Pan and I hoped that tinkerbell would die because shes like my sister.

Guy aged 6

Once you've had a baby you can't put it back.

Andrea aged 6

My father has a cros face

in the hokedays.

Jean aged 7

my daddy does love
me But he Is
very Buzy makeing
money.

David aged 7

My budgie broke is neck.
It served him rite because
he was always kissing himself
in the mirrer.

Tim aged 6

My dog had lots of babies
when he was young but when
he got old he just bit people

Martin aged 7

father christmas
and jesus are
best friends

Darryl aged 6

MY CAT HATES
BABIES BECAUSE.
THEY DRINK HiS MILK

Cathy aged 6

They told me to bow to the Alter but he wasnt there. I think he'd gone out with the vicar.

Emma aged 7

When you go to heaven you have to say sorry to the holy gost for not beleeving in him.

I dont beleeve in gosts so Im not goin there.

Kim aged 7

vikars dont larf mllch.
I Think its vecarge Jesus
didnt Tell many Jokes

Richard aged 6

I think Gods silly because he shoud have painted everybody the same colour and then they wouldnt fight.

Ricardo aged 7

God had lots of children but he never married which he shood have done

Enid aged 6

Baby Jesus was born with a yellow hat on and
3 Kings came to arsk her hand in marage and
they browt her lots of presents. Sarah aged 5

I dont like to see old ladies and men getting married becaus thayre to old for it

Dino aged 6

It is silly to get Married before you are 12

Edward aged 6

OLd ladys arent reeLy oLd Ladys. Therejust pepel waringold cLothes.

Jamie aged 6

you should never love someone
you dont like much

Katy aged 7

when you marry a girl you have to
give her o best man

Richard aged 6

I LOVE YOU